A
Minute
in the
Morning

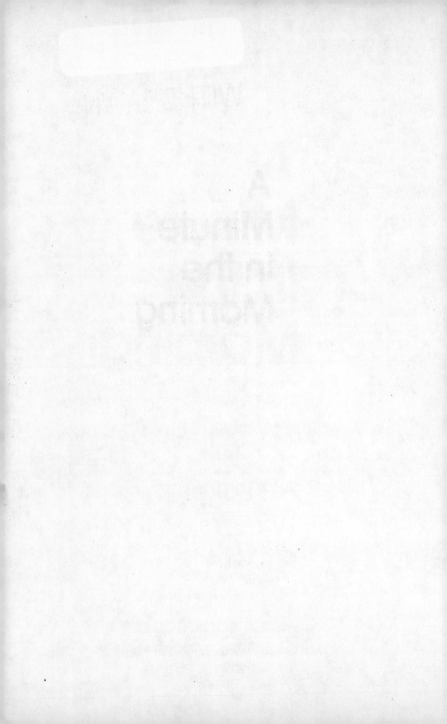

A Minute in the Morning

150 Devotions for Women

Pat Baker

BAKER BOOK HOUSE

Grand Rapids, Michigan 49506

Dedicated
to my sister
Jackie

We have shared many beautiful
moments together

Preface

You may never have felt that you could schedule a time during the day to be totally alone with God, but this book will prove to you that God can work wonders in your life if you give one minute each day to Him.

It will take you approximately one minute to read each meditation. It can become a guide to help you live out the twenty-four hours of the day. The words of God will come alive and vital, and you'll begin to look foward to claiming the promises from each verse. You'll discover the joy of living even when your outward circumstances seem hopeless and when those around you have lost their excitement for living even in the midst of God's perfect love.

The first chapter can give you the new beginning you're needing. As you spend these short times with Jesus, you will notice your life changing.

You are living in days of radical changes. Because so many noises surround you, you need some quiet, spiritual thoughts each morning to help you through the day. At times, life does become exhausting and the abundant life God has promised might seem to get lost in the complexity of your busy world. Reading this small book can give you the reassurance you need.

Take one minute to read a daily meditation, spend two minutes in prayer, and praise God for his loving-kindness. Then continue your day, knowing that God's presence will be with you.

Pat Baker

Contents

I

New Beginnings

Every morning tell him, "Thank you for your kindness," and every evening rejoice in all his faithfulness.

PSALM 92:2

1

Stand silent! Know that I am God! I will be honored by every nation in the world! PSALM 46:10

These are holy moments when you step aside from the world to be alone with God. In this stillness you can hear Him speak, because He is everywhere. It is the world, at times, that causes you not to hear. Can you sit quietly, turn your thoughts inward, and with a submissive spirit wait for that divine voice to give you today's assurance and instruction? When you seek God with a quiet mind and heart, you will learn to talk with Him, and He will be with you wherever this day leads you.

2

How precious it is, Lord, to realize that you are thinking about me constantly! I can't even count how many times a day your thoughts turn towards me. And when I waken in the morning, you are still thinking of me! PSALM 139:17-18

When you open your eyes to a new day, take a serious look at the events ahead of you. You can predict the difficulties that will be there. Some things are going to make you irritable, domineering, absorbed completely in your own desires, too busy to listen; but now, in this moment, take a good look, a long look at all these barriers and make up your mind to make them better. Look beyond yourself, even beyond your own struggles and the good you might perform in the lives of others. What needs does your husband or wife have? How can you help make this a better day for the children, the special friend who is having a difficult time, the person who took the time to send you a note that you hardly noticed? Now, at this time, you can stop and think of his finer traits, the unselfish life he has shared with you. Perhaps there is a hunger of his that you must help fill. It is good that you have had this quiet time to think about the goodness of all persons.

3

I will praise you, my God and King, and bless your name each day and forever.   PSALM 145:1-2

Try to have a quiet time at the beginning of each day. Before you leave your place of meditation, "commit your works" and everything you plan to do today to God. Commit those special things you have to do, the daily routines, and even the things that will come about unexpectedly, which God himself may choose to insert into your day. Think of all the things you want to accomplish. One by one, commit each action to God; offer all your thoughts, words, and actions to Him in order that each thing will be governed and guided by Him. Then throughout the day thank God for His perfect love and for the confidence He places in you as you strive to live through Him.

4

Into your hand I commit my spirit. PSALM 31:5

It may seem impossible at first, in the midst of a busy day, but try to be perfectly still in your mind and spirit. Get away from your own thoughts and turn your mind to God, who gave you life and your very being. In following this you will receive His strength and power to carry you through all of life's upsets. You will not be trying to live your life in your own strength. Do not dwell on your searchings, desires, and imaginations, but keep your mind fixed on God. You will find strength in Him, and you will know He is always at hand. He will be your constant help in time of trouble and need.

5

Yes, Lord, I'm listening. I SAMUEL 3:9*b*

In this moment, discipline your whole being to go before God in true humility, purity, and calmness. The silence will help you seek God's will for your life this day. If you will not think more of yourself than you ought to think, not look after your own interests only but others' welfare too, if you prepare yourself to accept all things as God's, then you will have a chance to benefit from what God has to tell you. During the devotions of one particular religion, the person puts his hands to his ears as if to listen for messages from the spiritual world. This is the attitude you must take in order to stand above the confusion of the mortal world.

6

I am quiet now before the Lord.   PSALM 131:2a

Be like a child today, content with the pleasure God gives you. Do not continually seek great things, but accept small gifts from God. These are the sweet beginnings of life. In becoming a child you must begin losing your own will and start accepting God's love and purpose in your life. Wait for your life to be measured out by God, and be content with the portion He hands you. When pleasure is gone and sorrow enters for a while, rest quietly in God; be patient and secure in His loving, most powerful arms.

7

That is why we never give up. Though our bodies are dying, our inner strength in the Lord is growing every day.

II CORINTHIANS 4:16

Sometimes in an attempt to provide comfort for your family, the stillness of your spirit may feel disturbed. It could be that you have started your work for the day without seeking God's guidance in order to know the direction of God's purpose in your life for that day. So many things seem to crowd in one's day that these quiet moments are often neglected. Something else you must learn to guard against is planning so much in one day that you over-fatigue yourself in

14

your daily work, because then you cannot give yourself freely to the needs of others and to the work you are to do. If you can be pleasant and speak quietly, it will make your family happier than anything else you can do for them. It is a fact that a person's own selfish will gets in the way of his duties sometimes. Let your inner being be renewed by a conversation with God in this moment.

8

For God wants you to be holy and pure.   I THESSALONIANS 4:3

Today, in the presence of God, try to come to terms with what you are really like. Then think about the purpose God has for you. Have you fulfilled His will, or are there other jobs He wants you to do now? What can you do today to obtain His approval? Ask for His help. "Help me to do your will, for you are my God" (Ps. 143:10). He will assure you of this request and say, "Fear not, I am thy salvation." He will give you peace; He will show you opportunities, and as He is doing these, He will show you glimpses of His own eternal love.

9

Don't worry about anything; instead, pray about everything; tell God your needs and don't forget to thank him for his answers.
PHILIPPIANS 4:6

Try praying until prayer makes you forget your own wishes and blend them into God's will. If your prayer does not succeed in keeping your desires to a minimum, in changing your desires into submission,

15

your anxious expectations into surrender, you have not prayed in a true spirit. God gives you prayer, not just to help you obtain the riches of this earth, but to learn to do without them. He doesn't ask you to pray in order to escape troubles, but prayer is a means to becoming strong enough to meet your troubles triumphantly.

10

Remember, your Father knows exactly what you need even before you ask him! MATTHEW 6:8

Are you aware of your needs for today? Do you know how to pray for your needs? As you go before the Father, let Him give daily to you power, work, fears, troubles He sees fit for you to have. His blessings will be over and above all that you could ever imagine. He will grant you mercy, grace, and hope, if with all your heart you seek Him and His righteousness above all else. These are the things your body needs—peace, comfort, joy, and His arms about you, assuring this promise to you that if you seek Him first, "all these other things shall be added unto you."

11

And may you be able to feel and understand, as all God's children should, how long, how wide, how deep, and how high his love really is; and to experience this love for yourselves, though it is so great that you will never see the end of it or fully know or understand it. And so at last you will be filled up with God himself. EPHESIANS 3:18-19

How does a person try Christianity? To admire its martyrs is not to try Christianity. You do not have to compare the teachings of Christianity with other religions. You do not have to attend various rituals to know Christianity. But if for one blessed hour you can experience living in faith and learning the matchless love of God, His tenderness toward you, His will in your life, and His eternal friendship, you have not only sought but also have found Christianity.

II

One Day at a Time

So don't be anxious about tomorrow. God will take care of your tomorrow too. Live one day at a time.

MATTHEW 6:34

1

I will trust and not be afraid, for the Lord is my strength and song; he is my salvation.

ISAIAH 12:2b

Try to live a simple life. Do not complicate your days with activities and thoughts that aren't necessary. Do not try so hard to have a quiet mind, and strangely enough it will become quieter. Do not crave to be perfect, but let your spiritual life be formed by your responsibilities, no matter how small they might seem. Do not always think about what you might do tomorrow. God has led you safely until now, and he will lead you on to the end. Hold to the promise that you are being kept in the everlasting confidence that you ought to have in God's heavenly providence.

2

I am holding you by your right hand—I, the Lord your God—and I say to you, Don't be afraid; I am here to help you.

ISAIAH 41:13

When changes come into your life or when you take a chance, don't be afraid; remember that since you are

God's child, He will sustain you. He will always keep you in His hands. All He asks of you is to hold his hand, and He will lead you safely through everything. When you don't feel that you can stand under the load, He will lift you in his mighty arms. A new day is more meaningful if you don't dwell on what might happen tomorrow. The everlasting Father who takes care of you today will take care of you tomorrow. God shields you from suffering or gives you the strength to overcome it.

3

You must lend him what he needs, and don't moan about it either! For the Lord will prosper you in everything you do because of this!   DEUTERONOMY 15:10

Many times you schedule your day to involve impossible achievements for twenty-four hours. Try to look on all interruptions to your work as discipline, sent by God to help you from getting selfish about your own work. Then feel that your true work, your work for God, consists of doing some seemingly trifling thing that has been thrown into your day. It is not a waste of time. It could become the part you can best offer to God. If you have an interruption, do not rush back to the schedule you had planned earlier that day; trust that the time to finish it will be given at another time.

4

The Lord will work out his plans for my life—for your lovingkindness, Lord, continues forever. Don't abandon me—for you made me.   PSALM 138:8

Do you get too busy with things in the future? The future is not yours. If this were so, it may be that you are running interference with the One to whom the future belongs when you attempt to dispense of it, wish it away, fill it up with your selfish desires and wild imaginations. In doing God's will you might find it necessary to go to Him hourly, possibly each moment, to learn exactly what He requires of you. Get out away from yourself, your friends, your interests, and trust that the path He has marked for your life will lead to your perfection and to God. This is your duty, so why shouldn't you try to walk every moment in a plain, simple, and uncomplicated way?

5

But life is worth nothing unless I use it for doing the work assigned me by the Lord Jesus.   ACTS 20:24

Today, think only of your present situation. Do not let your mind wander into the future. The future is not yours; perhaps it never will be. By thinking too far ahead you may expose yourself to temptation and may anticipate happenings that God may never intend for you. If these things would ever come to pass, be assured that He will give you strength according to your needs. There is no reason to try to meet difficulties prematurely when you do not have the strength or the knowledge that you will need. What *present* duties are there?

6

You alone are my God; my times are in your hands.

PSALM 31:15

Do not be in a hurry to choose your way of living today; wait to be guided. You are to be led like little children in a way that has not been completely revealed to you. It would not be right for you to try to get away from the work God intends for you to do in order to find a greater blessing. There is no other way to find the satisfying presence and peace of our divine Lord than to go to him daily in loving obedience.

7

Be glad for all God is planning for you. Be patient in trouble, and prayerful always. ROMANS 12:12

It is good to be patient with everyone, but above all, be patient with yourself. Don't be continually disturbed because your life isn't perfect. Take each day to try to improve on your imperfections. It is good to claim the promise that you have new beginnings each day. There is no better way to measure the progress of your spiritual life than to find new beginnings and never to think that you have done enough. Determination to improve is difficult, even when supported by the grace of God. New beginnings are the life of determination.

8

Yes, be bold and strong! Banish fear and doubt! For remember, the Lord your God is with you wherever you go. JOSHUA 1:9

Try not to let future things disturb you. Don't look at that mountain or river in the distance and keep saying, "How will I ever get over it?" But keep to your present task which is immediately before you and accomplish it. That task belongs to that moment. That mountain and that river can only be passed in the same way.

When you come to them, you will receive the strength that belongs to *that* moment.

9

Since the Lord is directing our steps, why try to understand everything that happens along the way? PROVERBS 20:24

Do you ever complain when life seems too slow and dull, when you feel you are in a low position in society, when you think you are "unknown," when you are wasting energy doing menial tasks? You may, in a way, be saying that you do not have a Father who is directing your life. He has forgotten you, so you decide on your own what is best. In your complaining, you lose the use of those quiet, slow years. Just because you are not sent out to do a certain work, should you even think that God has forgotten you? Just because you have been forced to become inactive for a while, don't you think that these quiet times cause you to be more conscious of doing your Father's business? This is a gift of time, given to you to prepare you for the work God will give to you eventually.

10

Bring joy to him who invited you into his kingdom to share his glory. I THESSALONIANS 2:12

It may take all the self-discipline you have, but accept, totally, the place that God has provided for you, the society in which you live, and the events that come into your life. You can find ways to adapt to things that happen in your life. Love every person your life touches. Do not be dissatisfied with your present life, neither fear your future. Each thing has its own season. Believe that you have been born into this world at just the right time. You are here to fulfill a definite purpose or God would not have seen fit for you to be born.

11

Are you seeking great things for yourself? Don't do it! . . . I will protect you wherever you go, as your reward.   JEREMIAH 45:5

Learn to be content. Try not to be too wise, overeager in your own will, rushing to try to satisfy your selfish desires. Living in this way will keep you from understanding the knowledge of the One who is your guide. He is the one who can lead you step by step. He can teach you how to follow. Begin contemplating, in this quiet moment, the holiness and goodness of God. Be still, and wait for the strength needed for this day that can only come through God's wisdom.

12

Now we are no longer slaves, but God's own sons. And since we are his sons, everything he has belongs to us, for that is the way God planned.   GALATIANS 4:7

At every hour of the day you have certain works to perform. You can do them negligently or faithfully like a trusting servant. Even if your daily work seems small and insignificant to you, do it well. You may consider yourself a person who is high or low, learned or unlearned, with a group of people or alone, or with numerous activities to fill your day. No matter what your circumstances, you have an opportunity to show affection, obedience, love, and mercy. The only thing that makes one person different from another is not so much what he does, but the way he does it. Use the hours of each day and the strength given you by the work of the Holy Spirit.

13

And now may the God of peace, who brought again from the dead our Lord Jesus, equip you with all you need for doing his will.   HEBREWS 13:20

What work is facing you today? Refer everything that you wish to accomplish to God. Offer your work to God; do each thing for Him, and He will be with you in all things. Nothing will interfere with you, but, rather, you will be inviting God's presence into your day. See Him in all things. This majesty can help you maintain peace in your home life. His love will sustain the serenity of your mind and give you a ready spirit of patience. If you have this, even the work that might seem to be a drudgery to you will be changed into something great and useful in the kingdom of God.

14

Just to follow hour by hour
As He leadeth;
Just to draw the moment's power
As it needeth.
F. R. HAVERGAL

Do you have disagreeable work to do at noon today? Do not let it affect the hours in between. Do the work that each hour calls for. Then when the dreaded hour comes, you can meet it and overcome it. This will keep your living full of light, and you will perform the right action. You will say the right words, and you will be so filled with the Holy Spirit that you cannot help doing what is right. When you can fully practice living one day at a time, the more peaceful your life will become, for you will continually rest in His unchanging grace.

15

So don't be anxious about tomorrow. God will take care of your tomorrow too. Live one day at a time.   MATTHEW 6:34

Today is yours; enjoy the blessings of it. Only this day is yours. Yesterday is gone and you do not have the promise of tomorrow. If you look too far ahead and think of things that will be and that will never be, your load may seem too unbearable and unreasonable.

Dear Lord, you have given me the blessings of beginning a new day. I do not know all that will occur today, but in this moment I want to lift myself unreservedly into thy matchless grace and care. If I do this, I know I shall receive the enjoyment which you intended this day to have. I have experienced yesterday, and tomorrow remains a mystery. Use me, God, to receive the beauty of this lovely day. Amen.

16

If you belong to the Lord, reverence him; for everyone who does this has everything he needs.   PSALM 34:9

Do you feel that anxiety over possible consequences ever made your judgment seem clearer or made you any wiser or braver about meeting your present needs? Pray for this day's needs only and leave tomorrow's needs to themselves. Don't form all the days together; leave them to the future. The events of your tomorrows will be met whether you anticipate them or not. Search to find a simple and honest way of living, and a capacity to work and enjoy it. Isn't that what God intended for His creation? One day at a time, Lord, teach me to live one day at a time. Amen.

17

I will be with you constantly until I have finished giving you all I am promising. GENESIS 28:15b

> Be quiet, soul:
> Why shouldst thou care and sadness borrow,
> Why sit in nameless fear and sorrow,
> The livelong day?
> God will mark out thy path to-morrow
> In His best way.
>
> ANONYMOUS

The best place for you is where God puts you. Any other place would be undesirable because it would only please you and would be *your* choice. Do not think about future events. It will cause you to become uneasy. Leave to God the things that depend on Him, and concentrate on being faithful in all that depends on you. If God takes away anything He has given you, be assured that He knows how to replace it, either through some other means or by Himself.

26

18

Teach us to number our days and recognize how few they are;
help us to spend them as we should.   PSALM 90:12

Each day renew your consecration to God's service, and turn away from anything that would grieve the Holy Spirit. God does not ask you to carry tomorrow's burdens or next week's or next year's. Every day ask Him to help you through this one day and the next day and the next and the next. Always leave your future in God's hands, because He can care for you much better than you can care for yourself. This moment is yours. You have specific work to do. The next moment is God's, and when it comes, His presence will come with it.

19

Not that I was ever in need, for I have learned how to get along
happily whether I have much or little.   PHILIPPIANS 4:11

Rules for a contented life:
1. Don't complain about anything, even the weather.
2. Don't let your imagination create situations that will never happen.
3. Don't compare your life with that of another.
4. Never dwell on the fact that if this or that had happened things wouldn't be as they are now. God loves you better and more wisely than you love yourself.
5. Don't think about tomorrow. Remember, tomorrow is God's, not yours.
   God's love will provide you with all things.

20

What does the Lord your God require of you except to listen carefully to all he says to you, and to obey for your own good the commandments I am giving you today, and to love him, and to worship him with all your hearts and souls?

DEUTERONOMY 10:12

Every day give yourself completely to God; meet every happening as something that comes from God. Seriously measure what it is God is asking you to do, and then go to work to fulfill your task with all your strength. What is beyond this daily calling is not yours to know. You will receive peace, quiet, confidence, and strength if you follow this simple daily rule.

21

Though the rain comes in torrents, and the floods rise and the storm winds beat against his house, it won't collapse, for it is built on rock.   MATTHEW 7:25

No one ever fell under the burden of one day. It is when you add tomorrow's burden to today's that the load is heavier than you can bear. If you find yourself with this added burden, remember it is your own doing and not God's. He pleads with you to leave the future to Him and to take care of the things in the present. Cast *all* your burdens upon God; hand them over completely, and He will sustain you.

22

He will not break the bruised reed.   ISAIAH 42:3a

God never gives you more than you can bear. You are always able to endure the present hour. If it were possible to gather up all your trials through many years, they would overwhelm you. Since your strength could not overcome all at one time, God sends one, then another. He removes these and may send another perhaps heavier than the first two, but He wisely measures your burdens with your strength so that the bruised reed is never broken. Each trial is meant to teach you something, although you may not realize it at the time. Trials are lessons which are beyond the power of anyone to teach alone.

23

Live one day at a time. MATTHEW 6:34*b*

Never fix your daily schedule to try to do more work than you can accomplish calmly, quietly, and without hurrying. If you have planned too busy a day and find yourself getting nervous, stop, take a deep breath. This very simple exercise could do more for you than prayers or tears of frustration could ever do. As soon as you realize that you are working with God in faith and in love, you are in prayer.

God, you have breathed life into my body. May my very breath be a living reminder of your blessed presence every moment of my life. Amen.

III

Praise

Oh, what a wonderful God we have! How great are his wisdom and knowledge and riches! How impossible it is for us to understand his decisions and his methods!

ROMANS 11:33

1

Make everyone rejoice who puts his trust in you. PSALM 5:11a

There is a gentle stroke of God's love that I see when I look up through the blossoms of a tree, when I listen to a bird that has built his nest among those branches. Then I look beyond the trees to the blue depths of the sky and feel it overshadow me with blessings. I realize it is the roof of the house of my Father, and if clouds choose to pass over it, there is still that unchangeable light beyond the clouds. When the day passes into night, it only unveils a new world of light. If it were possible to see beyond this universe, I would be unfolding rich blessings and seeing more deeply into the love at the heart of all grateful, abundant living.

2

Always be joyful. Always keep on praying. No matter what happens, always be thankful, for this is God's will for you who belong to Christ Jesus. I THESSALONIANS 5:16-18

Gratitude is taking note of your circumstances and being conscious of God's endless gifts in your life. You become aware that God truly loves and cares for you, even to the smallest, most trivial need in your life. It is a blessed thought to know that when you were a young child, even then God was watching over you. He speaks to you and brings down blessings from above, and you in turn respond with thanksgiving. Your whole life is drowned in the brightness of His holy countenance and is filled with unspeakable, indescribable gladness, tranquility, and peace which can only be known by a person with a thankful heart.

3

You have endowed him with eternal happiness. You have given him the unquenchable joy of your presence.   PSALM 21:6

Have you ever had a day when the sky seemed unusually brighter, the earth fairer, and the day more beautiful as it slipped into night? You have known many beauties—family ties, friendship, young love, music, art. You have looked into the blue sky which looked so deep and peaceful, so full of majesty that it seemed you could see the face of God. With all these daily surroundings of beauty, you will never experience the highest joy until you can actually see God in the universe. Always look for His light of infinite love and wisdom; see it shining over the world.

4

Glory in the Lord; O worshipers of God, rejoice. Search for him and for his strength, and keep on searching! PSALM 105:3, 4

I do not know when I have had happier times in a personal communion with God than when I have been by myself in a dark room with only the glimmer of soft candlelight, hearing only the sound of my breath, and knowing God was with me. I can rejoice in being exactly what I am and in being in love with who I am—a person capable of loving God and being assured that He loves me in return. When I look out the window and see the moon and stars, I know it is the work of the almighty hand of God. "For in him we live, and move, and have our being" (Acts 17:28 KJV).

5

There are many ways in which God works in our lives, but it is the same God who does the work in and through all of us who are his.   I CORINTHIANS 12:6

Every seasonal change, everything that touches your mind or body, whether brought on by nature or by the will of man, good or bad, is overruled by the all-loving will of God. No matter what comes your way, you must receive it as God's will. If the least thing could happen to you without God's permission, it would seem to be out of God's control. Then God's love, a love that has no human limits, would not be what He claims it to be. He would not be the same God, the God whom you have come to believe in, adore, and love with every extremity of your soul.

6

I have loved you, O my people, with an everlasting love; with lovingkindness I have drawn you to me.   JEREMIAH 31:3b

If all the human love you ever possess were tender, self-sacrificing, and devoted, if it could make you willing to abandon yourself for its sake, what can the divine love of God be like? Try to put together all the love you know or have ever felt and the strongest kind of love you have ever experienced and add to this all the loving human hearts in the entire world, multiply it by eternity, and you will begin to have an idea of the kind of love God has for you and for all His creation.

7

God knows you through and through. There is not one thought that is hidden from Him. As you come to know yourself, you come to see yourself more as God sees you. By doing this, you are able to catch a glimpse of His plan for your life; you know how each act of His checks out with your desires, your failures, and your hopes. Each situation is fitted just for you. These actions will affect your spiritual state. Until you come to this knowledge you must accept each experience in faith, believing that God is showing His goodness toward you. As you begin to know and accept yourself, you will, in a more complete way, know and accept God. It is so important to believe in the worth of your life.

8

I am radiant with joy because of your mercy, for you have listened to my troubles and have seen the crisis in my soul.
Yes, I will bless the Lord and not forget the glorious things he does for me.
PSALM 103:2

In every day God inserts surprises into your life to make the day seem a little more special. He adds this extra ingredient to your cup until it actually runs over with matchless blessings. There may be success in a business transaction that you were not counting on. The sound of a special song in the middle of drudgery, a glimpse of the early morning sky, a sunset that emerges before you as you rush to finish your day's work, a word of encouragement comes from someone; there are hundreds of other serendipities in life. Some may call them chance. Some may be identified as human kindness. But they are always God's love, for that kind of love is in every act of goodness. These small welcomed interruptions of yours are His ways of sharing His grace. These are His free gifts to you, His child.

9

The one thing I want from God, the thing I seek most of all, is the privilege of meditating in his Temple, living in his presence every day of my life, delighting in his incomparable perfections and glory. PSALM 27:4

Today, look closely at all that your eyes see. Everything that comes into focus has come from the Spirit which is the source of all external beauty. That beautiful blue sky is made by God, the great trees, all species of flowers, the moon, the stars, the heavens, the streams, the mountains—all of these that you are privileged to see are made and given to you by God. Look at people—all made by God. Oh, how your heart must rejoice at the thought of the eternal God, who is the origin of all things beautiful.

10

You must love the Lord your God with all your heart, and with all your soul, and with all your strength, and with all your mind. And you must love your neighbor just as much as you love yourself.   LUKE 10:27

O God, what offering shall I give
    To Thee, the Lord of earth and skies?
My spirit, soul, and flesh receive,
    A holy, living sacrifice.
                              JOACHIM LANGE

Try loving God "with all your heart." If you can begin doing this, you will experience a spiritual passion of gratitude for loving kindness. To love Him "with all your mind" will be to have a love for beauty that inspires you to put your very soul into your work. To love Him "with all your soul" is to know complete devotion and will cause you to look into the face of God. To love Him "with all your strength" is the spiritual passion that tests all the rest—knowing reality, worshiping in spirit and truth, being what you feel you must be, and doing what you know God's word wants you to be.

11

For you have stored up great blessings for those who trust and reverence you.   PSALM 31:19b

You do not have to look toward the sky to find God, but recognize this fact: He *is* the universe. He is separate from no place or thing. He reveals himself in all things and in all events, moment by moment. He is eternal. God will always be present, always new. You will adore Him and gratefully receive Him abundantly in the events each moment brings. You are never and will never be away from Him, and He will never be away from you. He will always be "a very present help" (Psalm 46:1b KJV).

12

May the Lord bless and protect you; may the Lord's face radiate with joy because of you; may he be gracious to you, show you his favor, and give you his peace.   NUMBERS 6:24-26

When your faith in God seems perfectly clear and you grasp His will and purpose, then you can begin to live more confidently. You will be patient and keep your composure even in times of trouble. You will feel a communion with God and you will sense your very soul in the presence of God. You distinctly experience a holy reverence that you cannot describe. You will have this from time to time with God—not often—but when you do you will look at God, man, the earth, the heavens, and stand in awe as you catch a fleeting glimpse of the greatness of the almighty Creator.

13

I have called you by name; you are mine.   ISAIAH 43:1b

God sees you as an individual. He calls you by name. He sees you and understands you. He knows your feelings, your thoughts, your disposition, your strengths, and your weaknesses. He sees you on the days when you rejoice and on the days when you experience sorrow. He is interested in your anxieties. You cannot possibly love yourself more than God loves you. If pain is brought upon you to bear, He will be with you; and if you are wise enough, you will see a greater good come from the pain that will make you a stronger person, full of hope and glory.

14

Jehovah is constantly thinking about us and he will surely bless us . . . and all, both great and small, who reverence him.

PSALM 115:12, 13

Cherish this one thought: God is near you *all* the time, watching, seeing your good intentions before He sees your failures. He knows your desires before He sees your faults. He helps you endeavor to do great things, yet accepts the least of your service for Him. But above all, He is content with your meager love. Remember this wherever or whatever you are, even though you lead a simple and weak life, you love Him no less than the busiest, strongest, most gifted person. If He is your sovereign Lord, loved above all else, then not much else matters. Whatever concerns you He will perfect in His own stillness and in His matchless power.

15

For I cried to him and he answered me! He freed me from all my fears.   PSALM 34:4

If you cannot seem to find a remedy for your troubles, turn to the Lord often today. Though you feel like an insignificant being, He is watching over you in your work and distractions. He will send you help and bless your life. Raise your voice and very soul to God; ask for His help. Your annoyances will be unimportant when you realize you have a friend in Jesus, a refuge in time of trouble, and a lover of your soul. Pray, in this moment, that you will feel God's presence in your life and go about your work and decision-making, knowing He will not fail you.

16

For in Him we live and move and are!   ACTS   17:28a

Where is God? You say, "He is everywhere. He is everlasting." When has He been with you? You believe He is ready to help you when you are tempted, and He will lift you up when you have fallen. When did you experience His grace in those hours? In your sorrow could you find joy? These questions may help you measure how you feel about the unlimited power of the almighty God. Worship Him, commune with Him, and prove to yourself that He is the God in whom we live and move and have our being.

17

We live within the shadow of the Almighty, sheltered by the God who is above all gods.   PSALM   91:1

"There shall no evil befall thee, neither shall any plague come nigh thy dwelling" is a promise that will always be fulfilled for everyone "who dwells in the secret place of the Most High." Sorrows will not seem like evils, sickness will not be plagues, because the shadow of God extends completely around the person who lives under that shadow and alters the character of every happening which comes within its influence. Faith's work is to claim and challenge loving kindness out of all the acts of God.

18

And the Lord will guide you continually, and satisfy you with all good things, and keep you healthy too; and you will be like a well-watered garden, like an ever-flowing spring. ISAIAH 58:11

Trust God completely in all things. Even though it seems you are in the midst of a desert without anything but the sand and the heat of the day surrounding you and that you may have to make a long journey to arrive at green pastures, still, trust in Him to guide you. The Shepherd can turn the very place where you are into a serene, quiet pasture; for only He has the power to make the desert rejoice and burst forth as a rose. "He leadeth me beside the still waters."

19

He lets me rest in the meadow grass and leads me beside the quiet streams. He restores my failing health. He helps me do what honors him the most.   PSALM 23:2-3

God becomes a part of your life when you are obedient, devoted, and have a sustained faith in Him. He will guide you when things cause you to be weary, afraid, sad, lonely, and even when your closest friend does not realize you are facing trials. Yet, God remains sufficient for your needs. By his gentle voice He will guide you. By His rod and staff if you wander, and by every available means, He will guide you in all things.

20

God is our refuge and strength, a tested help in times of trouble. And so we need not fear even if the world blows up, and the mountains crumble into the sea.   PSALM 46:1-2

Your daily routines may change, work may take the place of rest, sickness may take the place of health, trials may be yours from within and without. Externally you are not free from life's circumstances; but if your life is fixed on God, no matter what the present may bring, just knowing that it is His will and that your future will be influenced by it, will make it not only tolerable but even welcomed by you. This kind of faith comes from knowing that the One who holds you in His powerful hands cannot change but lives with you forever.

21

How precious is your constant love, O God!   PSALM 36:7a

The eternal God is your Refuge,
And underneath are the everlasting arms.
                                      DEUTERONOMY 33:27a

"What a blessedness, what a peace is mine, leaning on the everlasting arms." When your husband puts his arms around you at the end of the day, when you sit with your child and put your arms around him, the day seems sweeter, and rest comes easier, because you stop to realize the strength of the almighty arms of God holding you—always. You can feel closer to God when you have this thought. Nothing is more tender than to know He holds you as a child, encloses and engulfs your very being. He is always filling this great earth and all things upon it with His indescribable, unseen force of love that never forgets anything or anyone and never exhausts itself so that every time you lean upon Him you can be comforted.

22

Look at me instead through eyes of mercy and forgiveness, through eyes of everlasting love and kindness.   PSALM   25:7*b*

You need to be assured that your sins are forgiven. How do you go about feeling that your life has been cleansed by God? How do you keep from feeling guilty after you have sinned? First, if you can, feel that you have peace with God. Feel that you are going to trust in the unlimited and divine tenderness of your Father. In that instant, when you have sinned, go to God and say, "Father I have done wrong, forgive me." Then open up your very soul to Him until He can completely fill it with His love. Wait on Him until you find peace. *Do not hurry.* Wait until your conscience no longer bothers you, until you can feel that your sin, great as it is, can never keep you away from your heavenly Father. Nothing "shall be able to separate us from the love of God, which is in Christ Jesus our Lord." Claiming this truth, go your way rejoicing in the grace of God.

23

Shall I not drink from the cup the Father has given me?

JOHN 18:11*b*

Think of the smallest sorrows and then of the greatest sorrows that God has allowed to take place in your life. All of these experiences have proceeded from the depths of His unspeakable love. If only you have a mild form of sickness or if you feel hungry or thirsty, if others have made you uneasy or angry by their words or actions, or whatever happens that causes you distress or pain, it will all help get you ready for greater works. You will have an abundant life because you have trusted each of your circumstances to the Lord.

24

He is beloved of God
And lives in safety beside him.
God surrounds him with his loving care,
And preserves him from every harm.

DEUTERONOMY 33:12

You must come to that place in life to say without any doubt that God gives you everything you need. You can get along without the things He denies you. Whether something is taken from you or is not given to you, sooner or later God satisfies you in himself without it. Learn to put all your concerns on the Lord and feel secure in the care and wisdom of the heavenly Father. When you stop to think about it, your life without God grows darker and darker each day. Even feeling this way, do not feel as though you distrust

God. By faith live just as content and satisfied in the absence of all things as you would if you possessed all things.

25

Won't your Father in heaven even more certainly give good gifts to those who ask him for them?   MATTHEW 7:11*b*

When you ask God for something that really isn't good for you, He will keep it back from you. He is not showing less love; He just doesn't grant you all your desires. If you pray haphazardly, not really knowing what you ask, you may be praying for things which will bring you sorrow. Because of God's love, He will deny you these things. It would be disastrous to have all your wishes turned into realities, your hasty wishes fulfilled, and all your capricious longings granted. There will come a day when you will praise God not for what He has granted you, but for what He has denied.

26

Their words sting like poisonous snakes.   PSALM   140:3

Sometimes you may be tempted to indulge yourself in disappointments, daily irritations, and weariness. You may find it a hard thing to meet your own family, your neighbors, and your friends. You might experience moods of discontent, preoccupation, impatience, ruthlessness, and ill health. In order to conceive that any man has accomplished the feat of being master of himself, you must realize that the graciousness of his power can only be fashioned after the style

43

of the Perfect Man. Only then can you genuinely accept yourself as you are—a person made in the image of God.

27

Oh, what a wonderful God we have! How great are his wisdom and knowledge and riches! How impossible it is for us to understand his decisions and his methods! ROMANS 11:33

If it is your greatest desire to lead a noble and holy life and you pray without ceasing to God for this kind of life, trying to be consistent in your desire, it will be granted to you, even if it does not come until the day you die. If God does not grant it to you now, you will find it in Him in eternity. So, do not grow weary if you feel your desire is not being filled. The love and aspiration you so deeply desire lives constantly before God. He honors those who honor Him.

IV

Peace

He will keep in perfect peace all those who trust in him, whose thoughts turn often to the Lord!   ISAIAH 26:3

1

Consider the lilies of the field, how they grow; they toil not, neither do they spin: And yet I say unto you, That even Solomon in all his glory was not arrayed like one of these.
MATTHEW 6:28-29 KJV

Do not look back in fear to that part of your life that is already past. Do not be anxious about the future, of which you know nothing and of which you are not even sure. Instead, have no will but God's will. An old man in his youth saw a little flower growing up between a horse's path and the wheel tracks of a wagon. He noticed that if the flower had grown just an inch more to the right or left, or grown any higher, it would not have been safe from the daily traffic. It bloomed as though it had hundreds of acres of space around it and never knew the danger there. It did not borrow trouble but grew more beautiful in spite of the place it bloomed. Will you trust the Lord as completely with your life?

2

Be humble and gentle. Be patient with each other, making allowance for each other's faults because of your love. Try always to be led along together by the Holy Spirit, and so be at peace with one another.   EPHESIANS 4:2-3

Every morning ask God to give you the kind of spirit that will enable Him to shape your life. Think of it a hundred times during the day, allowing God to see and know your efforts. In doing this you will subject your life entirely to His will, and very slowly you will become a gentle, loving, forgiving person, trusting completely in His goodness. It is a guarantee for happiness because you will begin to feel God in your life; and where God is, there is peace. If you should fail along the way and some of your old faults appear, do not be discouraged; continue to be assured that God is with you and is seeing you try.

3

Dear friends, don't be bewildered or surprised when you go through the fiery trials ahead, for this is no strange, unusual thing that is going to happen to you. Instead, be really glad—because these trials will make you partners with Christ in his suffering, and afterwards you will have the wonderful joy of sharing his glory in that coming day when it will be displayed.
                    I PETER 4:12-13

Try to receive every happening in your life—inward or outward trouble, disappointments, temptations, pain, uneasiness—as an opportunity for literally dying to the strength that is in your own body and completely entering into that full fellowship with the Savior. Discipline your thinking to look at no problem in any other view than this; turn away every thought about it, and you will be able to overcome. The state of your very existence is best when you exercise the highest kind of faith in God. Rest fully in the power that only God bestows upon those who love Him.

4

If I ride the morning winds to the farthest oceans, even there your hand will guide me, your strength will support me.

PSALM 139:9-10

How can you come to that place in life where you feel that God is leading you? Surely it is by carefully looking into your life and living within the limitations of your own soul. Be content and concentrate on stopping your restless search for outward things. Surrender yourself to God each day and follow Him wherever He leads you. He may ask you to take time to contemplate or cause you to act on a certain situation; he may want you to do something useful or for sheer enjoyment. You may be filled with great sorrow or abounding joy; in any event let Him lead you. If you cannot feel God's hand in all things, simply yield yourself to Him for His sake. In love, continue your life.

5

In quietness and confidence is your strength.　ISAIAH 30:15b

Could you try to see God in all things? Do everything for God. Do not be in a hurry, do your work that is before you, and do it with a calm spirit. Keep your inward peace, even if your whole world seems upset. Hand God everything in this moment and then be still and rest in Him. No matter what happens, be firm and determined to simply cling to God and to trust the eternal love He has for you. If you feel you have wandered from His shelter, call upon Him quietly and simply. Discipline yourself not to worry about so many cares, imaginings, wishes, or longings.

6

Dear friends, let us practice loving each other, for love comes from God and those who are loving and kind show that they are the children of God, and that they are getting to know him better.   I JOHN 4:7

Try to create within your life a spirit of love, for here lies the truth and reality of God in your soul. The greatest blessing that could ever be granted to you is God's living within your life. When this occurs, bitterness disappears; all wants are satisfied; living is no longer a burden; the day becomes peaceful. Everything you experience actually becomes a help to you, because everything you see or do is done in that sweet, gentle, unselfish act of love.

7

He will keep in perfect peace all those who trust in him, whose thoughts turn often to the Lord!   ISAIAH 26:3

God is a serene being. Because of this you must keep your spirit in the same way, and this same quality of serenity will live within you. If, at times, something causes you to worry or to become fearful or anxious, move away from it. There is nothing in this world worth losing your peace of mind over. Since God gives bountifully of joy and peace, endeavor to also have a continually joyful and peaceful way of living. Avoid those who irritate you, who cause you to be anxious, who grumble when things don't go their way. When you begin to feel these things bothering you, gently turn away from them and fill your life with good thoughts and true motives.

8

I waited patiently for God to help me; then he listened and heard my cry.   PSALM 40:1

Is it possible—when everything seems wrong, when you feel despair and you cannot seem to find happiness—to hold the conviction that God's mercy toward you is real, even when you have a heavy heart? He can lead you to peace. He will help you resist temptation; He will help you to be a useful person. He will help you give up your will and teach you to rejoice in God's will. From all these rich gifts, your life receives the force to go on living abundantly.

9

May all who are godly be happy in the Lord and crown him, our holy God.   PSALM 97:12

Nothing can bring about a greater serenity than a mind that is free from guilt. This will keep your soul undisturbed, and the end result will be to live justly, honestly, satisfied, fulfilled. When a shrub is cut down it retains its fragrance for a long time, so it is compared to the person whose actions are good and wise and leave a rich scent for others to enjoy. So let us number our days.

10

For if you stand firm, you will win your souls. LUKE 21:19

Your soul loses command of itself when you allow it to become impatient. When you become impatient, you begin to desire what you don't have or either you do not desire what you do have. You may possess all earthly wealth, but you will find that peace does not come from having material things, but it is what you have filled your soul with, that will last. You can have peace even in the midst of pain if your will remains firm and submissive. The pain you experience in most of your trials is not actually caused by going through the suffering, but it is caused when your spirit resists it.

11

So let it [your patience] grow, and don't try to squirm out of your problems. For when your patience is finally in full bloom, then you will be ready for anything, strong in character, full and complete. JAMES 1:4

To be patient involves a constant practice of the presence of God. You never know when you will be called upon to display patience. What might seem to be your private property, such as your time, home, rest, is constantly being invaded by trials of patience. Just within your home you have numerous occasions to practice patience. When you can master these under stress, remain gentle when you are being wronged, only then will you know the manner of spirit that is in Christ.

12

But they that wait upon the Lord shall renew their strength. They shall mount up with wings like eagles; they shall run and not be weary; they shall walk and not faint.　　ISAIAH 40:31

If you can, try living a submissive life under the guidance of the Holy Spirit. In doing this, you will become surrounded with internal pleasures greater than could ever be attained in this world. You will be able to increase the inward powers of your mind, and God will set your heart toward all the good purposes of life. Your soul will be filled with lasting pleasures.

13

Happiness comes to those who are fair to others and are always just and good.　　PSALM 106:3

When you find yourself in the darkest hour of life, be certain of this: cling to the things that can never fail you. Even if there were no God, no future state of being, it is still better that you be generous with your life and not selfish; it is better to be true to others and yourself instead of to be false; it is better to be brave and not a coward. When others bring trouble upon you, when friends seem to forsake you, hold fast to the faith that is within you. You will be immeasurably blessed when you are facing dreariness and cheerlessness from within and without. It is true, you will be blessed because the darkness you find within your soul that only God could explain, in this moment shall pass into a humanly unexplained clear, bright day.

14

Be silent, all mankind, before the Lord, for he has come to earth from heaven, from his holy home.   ZECHARIAH 2:13

God is always whispering to you, but you do not always hear because of noise, hurry, and distractions which daily living drowns out. Whenever the sounds begin to diminish, then you can hear the soft voice of God. As long as you allow a noisy restlessness of your thoughts to invade the quiet times, the gentle desires of God are overpowered and your life becomes inactive. Pray for a quiet look at the divine and eternal truth of God. Rest in the all-loving God, reject all the imaginings of your mind; calm your mind as you pause in the very presence of the Divine One and accept the strength that only He can give for day-to-day living.

15

But I want your will, not mine.   MATTHEW 26:39b

When you resign yourself to the will of God, not withholding any area of your life from Him, this act becomes the completeness of faith. This is the beauty of faith. In God's will is everything that is good. God can become the source of a quiet, composed mind. Resigning yourself to the will of God may be said to be perfect when your will is lost in His. There are never disappointments when your will is buried completely in the will of God.

16

The Lord is my light and my salvation; whom shall I fear?

PSALM 27:1

When trouble comes to you—whether of mind or body, from without or within, by chance or intent, from friends or enemies—whatever your trouble is, even though you feel very much alone, remember your heavenly Father and do not be afraid. Nothing can reach you to harm you when everything and everyone must first of all touch God who has completely enclosed you in His arms. God rejoices in you when, even though surrounded by insurmountable circumstances, you continue to love, adore, and praise God! Do not be afraid of anything. Your strength comes from within your soul, placed there only by the supreme power of God.

17

Nothing will ever be able to separate us from the love of God demonstrated by our Lord Jesus Christ when he died for us.

ROMANS 8:39b

Imagine your hands clasped between Christ's and God's. With this security, claim the promise that nothing in this mortal world will ever be able to pluck you out of his hands. Have the trials of today—sorrow, doubting, sickness—overcome you or seemed overwhelming; have no answers come through decisions you must make? No, not even these shall ever separate you from the love of God through Christ Jesus. Concentrate on the word *nothing* in this moment. "They that wait upon the Lord shall renew their strength" (Isa. 40:31a).

18

I will lift up mine eyes unto the hills, from whence cometh my help.   PSALM 121:1 KJV

How can you possibly live quietly in the midst of daily irritations, all the little worries which you cannot get away from? You cannot change your surroundings, so whatever kind of life you are to live must be lived right where you are. Being restless or discontent will not change anything. Make up your mind to accept what you cannot change. You can live a beautiful life in the midst of your present circumstances. Try to realize a state of inward happiness, totally independent of your circumstances.

19

If you are angry, don't sin by nursing your grudge. Don't let the sun go down with you still angry—get over it quickly; for when you are angry you give a mighty foothold to the devil.
                                                     EPHESIANS 4:26-27

Everyone is troubled by anger at times. When you feel you have been offended or when you become annoyed with someone, don't dwell on it or anything related to that situation. Instead, struggle against these frustrations and annoyances with patience, no matter how upsetting an event has been to you. God will bless your efforts if you truly try not to continue to have harsh feelings against the one who has offended you.

20

But when you are praying, first forgive anyone you are holding a grudge against, so that your Father in heaven will forgive you your sins too.   MARK 11:25

There is absolutely nothing you can do with a person but love him, admire his virtues, feel pity when he makes an error, forgive him when he causes you grief. Try to think of any other way to deal with a person you dislike, but you will never be able to find another way. You can hate him, but that will not help you. You might feel such hatred you could kill him, but that will not help you. Nothing in this vast universe can help you but to love him. How many misunderstandings could be solved by one simple word spoken to the one who has caused you trouble? Peaceful living can be yours if love is there; your darkness would be filled with light, your hatred turned to love. There is nothing in this world you can do with a person but love him.

21

You need to keep on patiently doing God's will if you want him to do for you all that he has promised.   HEBREWS 10:36

Patience: How often do you pray for it? It is one of the most beautiful virtues in living. Patience gives you contentment, keeps you from grumbling, keeps away selfish desires, smothers all anxious thoughts, and causes you to live quietly and submissively. You will begin to wait for the inward power of God which will then help to preserve your spiritual being and will make you vitally aware of your purpose for living.

22

A soft answer turns away wrath, but harsh words cause quarrels.
PROVERBS 15:1

It doesn't bother you quite so much to receive a hurt from someone as it does to remember the incident. A small hurt comes and goes; a greater one may stay with you longer, but be determined that none will be in your mind constantly. Don't lose the precious moments of each day because someone has hurt you. This will not benefit you in any way. Do not grieve about things in the past that cannot be corrected. Don't worry about things that cannot be prevented. Commit yourself to God now and in your future and then begin enjoying your present state of being.

23

Not that I speak in respect of want: for I have learned, in whatsoever state I am, therewith to be content.
PHILIPPIANS 4:11 KJV

God does not have to set you in different places, but He sometimes keeps you right where you are with just the right circumstances to surround you. Many times he transforms the very things that you thought were hindrances into things that will cause more spiritual growth to come about. There is not one difficulty that you will ever face that God cannot handle. There is nothing in your past that can mar the perfect work He plans to accomplish through you. All you are asked to do is to put yourself completely into His arms and let Him have His way with you.

V

Commitment

I would have you learn this great fact: that a life of doing right is the wisest life there is. If you live that kind of life, you'll not limp or stumble as you run. Carry out my instructions; don't forget them, for they will lead you to real living.   PROVERBS 4:11-13

1

So don't worry at all about having enough food and clothing. Why be like the heathen? For they take pride in all these things and are deeply concerned about them. But your heavenly Father already knows perfectly well that you need them, and he will give them to you if you give him first place in your life and live as he wants you to.   MATTHEW 6:31-33

Lord, I don't know what I should ask you. You are the only one who knows what I need. I come, in this moment, simply presenting myself before you. I want you to reveal all your purposes for me, even though it is not clear what they are. I offer myself completely; I yield myself to you now in your presence. I have no other desire today except to accomplish your will. Teach me to pray so you will be able to reveal to me your divine purposes. Amen.

2

And if God cares so wonderfully for flowers that are here today and gone tomorrow, won't he more surely care for you, O men of little faith?   MATTHEW 6:30

Give yourself up to the completeness of God's sweet control. Put your spiritual growth into His hands, as completely as you have put all your other interests of life. Let Him manage your life. Don't spend so much time trying to figure out His will, just put your absolute trust in Him. Accept each moment as it is given you from Him, as being the very thing you need for that moment's growth. Every time you feel anxious or get in a hurry or want your will to be done, you are preventing God from working with your life. Look at a flower. It opens its petals quietly, and the sun shines into that flower and uses its gentle influence to help it grow and bloom. God will do this for you when you yield yourself to Him.

3

This is the day the Lord has made. We will rejoice and be glad in it.   PSALM 118:24

You will never obtain gentle peace until you have performed the greatest duty of all—until you have presented yourself to your Father. You can receive the greatest joys by performing the smallest duties in this moment. There will be small cares coming up during each day; you will find your life deficient in some areas; your mind will not react clearly in quick decisions. You may find these cares threatening you and you may feel your soul has no freedom from these cares. Let God remain superior in your life, be ready at every call, and be thoroughly furnished unto all good works.

4

And I am sure that God who began the good work within you will keep right on helping you grow in his grace until his task within you is finally finished on that day when Jesus Christ returns. PHILIPPIANS 1:6

Any Christian who gives himself completely to God, will be kept safe. What keeps you from fully realizing this truth? Do you need strength? You actually have all the strength you need from the Holy Spirit. Do you limit His power? Did you ever begin a particular work that you knew without a doubt was God's will for you to be doing and then fail because you didn't have enough strength? Try to embrace God with all the love you have; hold to it. Many times you open only certain areas of your will to be influenced by the divine will. You are afraid to be completely absorbed in this will. And yet, if you will only stop to think that if you really desire peace in living, you must be completely united with God.

Lord, if I have never done it until now, I want you to know I want to be completely, totally yours in order to perform the works you have sent me to do. Amen.

5

Tell me what to do, O Lord, and make it plain. PSALM 27:11

God alone knows how to lead you in this life. Believe that He knows every aspect of your soul, every thought you have, every secret you try to hide, all your difficulties, and the things that seem to give you trouble. He knows how each event, each trial, each temptation will affect you, and He takes care of you in each instance. If you can fully grasp this belief in your mind, soul, and body, it will influence your entire life. There will be no question that you will submit yourself to God more readily. You will not ask for anything, wish for anything, refuse anything, except what He wills. You will take all he sends you without question and believe that one day at a time is enough for you to handle. You will feel satisfied even though your way may seem dark. God is directing you all the way, and what seems a hindrance in your life might prove to be a blessing, because God wills it.

6

Don't copy the behavior and customs of this world, but be a new and different person with a fresh newness in all you do and think. Then you will learn from your own experience how his ways will really satisfy you.   ROMANS 12:2

There are some steps which lead to the holiness of living, which set you apart and free you from burdens, and which cause you to rejoice in the constant hope that is in you as a Christian. God does not want you to become anxious about any happenings, take part in disputes, or participate in idle talk which may tear down the character of another. He might have you to rearrange your life more simply and not use up your precious time searching after what you cannot obtain in this earthly life. When the world offers things contrary to His purpose, stop and wait to know God is working in your life and follow what is acceptable to Him. When your mind is seeking God's mind, true light and true living are given and readily received. Be calm in God in all your day's events.

7

You will be anxious to follow the example of those who receive all that God has promised them because of their strong faith and patience.   HEBREWS 6:12*b*

Practice living in hope today. Those Christians who have already left this earth were once like you. They were weak, had faults, sinned. They had burdens, were hindered; they became weary and they failed. Now they have overcome. Their lives were similar to yours. Their day was lived like yours. They saw sunrises and sunsets just as you do. They had their sad and lonely times. They had hours they wasted through worrying and disturbing changes. You experience nothing new from what they experienced. They overcame each thing as it was handed to them; each one had his turn and when the time came, God was there to help him. Your life can be like this by living it through Christ.

8

And I delight to do your will, my God, for your law is written upon my heart!   PSALM 40:8

What is devotion? You hear of people's being devoted to one another, to their jobs, to their homes, to their children. Devotion is nothing more than being ready to do what you feel is acceptable to God. It is that "free spirit" David was speaking of when he said, "I will run the way of thy commandments, when thou shalt enlarge my heart" (Ps. 119:32 KJV). Ordinary good people walk the way of God, but the devout person runs in it and at times seems to fly in it. To be a devout person, you must not only do God's will, but you must do it cheerfully and with love. God wants you to be delighted with the thought that He would even have you serve Him; it is your life that He asks of you.

9

For the Kingdom of God is within you.   LUKE 17:21*b*

God has assigned to you a special work—to have a meaningful, satisfying life, to make this world whatever it is capable of being, sufficient for God to reign with you, being thankful when you are permitted to build a life of grace, goodness, and holy love, a life compared to the temple of God. But if you are denied this privilege, resolve to let God reign so you will not become disobedient, distrustful, doubtful, and break your communion with Him. So whether you are happy or sorrowing, struggling with the injustice of circumstances or if you find yourself in an atmosphere of peace, in fellowship, or alone, your greatest desire can be that God may hold the complete realm of your life where obedience and submission are so you may experience communion of the spirit and an ever-loving trust with your Savior. This will make you able to receive the peace that passes all understanding.

63

10

Be careful to do good deeds all the time, for this is not only right, but it brings results.   TITUS 3:8*b*

It is impossible to live in close fellowship with God if you do not conceive of all your daily work as holy. If you do not accept the opportunities to help others, your profession of faith in God is simply dead. Do not quench the first beginnings of devotion. There is no way you can go from a quarrelsome, angry disposition, to God. If your selfish life, neglect, suspicions, and greed get the best of you, your life will be darkened and the face of God will be hidden from you. Go to God and ask for a cleansing of your soul today. It will cause you to fulfill your life and to be happy in the promise that He will renew a right spirit within you.

11

Give your burdens to the Lord. He will carry them.
PSALM 55:22*a*

There are certain circumstances in life that you cannot alter, but take them to the Lord, let Him manage them. Believe that He takes them and takes over total responsibility, worry, and anxiety with Him. Every time the anxiety reappears, again return them to God. Your circumstance may remain unchanged, but your soul will have perfect peace in the midst of all that occurs. This will not only affect your outward living but also your inward being. Give your whole self to the Lord with all you are and have; believe that He takes what you have committed to Him; stop worrying, and your life will become fulfilling, abundant, and satisfying, because you belong to Him.

12

I will make him a pillar in the temple of my God.

REVELATION 3:12*a*

In this world the temple of God is being erected. Anytime a person catches a glimpse of God's likeness, his life becomes a living stone in the edification of life. Maybe your fight for living right is hard; you become tired; you are tempted. But through these trials you realize the purpose of your being and give yourself to God. Then God takes charge of your life, makes it a living stone. In whatever way your life is being tried, God is there, shaping it for the pillars of his temple. What if today your life was one of these stones and you could have a vision of the kind of temple God is building? What patience you must possess when you know that the success of the temple depends completely on letting yourself be fashioned into the shape the Master wills.

13

And he said, The things which are impossible with men are possible with God.   LUKE 18:27 KJV

Your mind is a very complex part of your physical makeup. It puts forth its greatest power when you are experiencing a trial, if it calmly yields its desires, affections, and interest to God. There are times when to be still demands greater discipline on your part than to act upon a given situation. Being composed is often the result of power. To see power in action is to witness a man who has been stripped of all his belongings, lost all he has ever held of value, and then very quietly returned to the work which God assigned to him.

14

Don't be discouraged. Don't be upset. Expect God to act!
PSALM 42:11a

Do not let your cares cause you to be anxious. Say to God, "Oh, God, I am looking to you for help. Guide me and teach me *your* way of life." After you have offered this prayer, be comforted. You can go successfully through all of life's situations if your heart is right, your intentions are pure, and you have your courage and trust in God. Sometimes you may be overwhelmed by circumstances; you will become uneasy about small worries. Consider these things as opportunities for strengthening your character and accept the grace that God gives you so generously.

15

Obey me and I will be your God and you shall be my people;
only do as I say and all shall be well!
JEREMIAH 7:23

Ask God to give you an honest and good heart, and without any hesitation start to obey him with the best heart you have. Any kind of obedience is better than none at all. Every work you have to do is an obedience. To do what God asks you to do is to obey Him. Each time you obey you are approaching Him as the Lord of your life, the one who gave you life from the start. Obedience is an approach that is not far off, even though at times it may seem He is following you at a far distance. By laying yourself at his complete disposal you will have sufficient light to guide your way. There is no groping for anything when God is with you.

16

Never be lazy in your work but serve the Lord enthusiastically.
ROMANS 12:11

You may find it true that you cannot be a useful or comforting person if you cannot find it in your heart to be kind. If your spirit chooses to continually find fault, if you have an uncontrolled temper, if you cannot even be content with the weather, daily blessings, friends, and health, these complaints will more than neutralize all the good you could do. They will keep you from making life a blessing to yourself and others. No one can fulfill any duty without first fulfilling the act of being pleasant.

17

You should be like one big happy family, full of sympathy toward each other, loving one another with tender hearts and humble minds.   I PETER 3:8

Today, think how your own happiness depends upon the way you look at and live with other people. Begin with the looks and moods at the breakfast table, the way your fellow workers conduct themselves, the faithful or unreliable persons you must deal with, what people say to you, the friends or enemies you meet—these things will cause you to receive pleasure or misery today. Then remember that you, too, are either adding pleasure or misery to other people's day. This is the part that *you* control. You, only you, will determine what days will bring you happiness or unhappiness. You must decide whether each day of your life will give you the joys that will help you enjoy your salvation. It is left entirely up to you.

67

18

You must do everything for the glory of God.

I CORINTHIANS 10:31*a*

Everything that fills your day—the things that are right for you—is part of your obedience to God; it is a part of your religion. When you hear people complain about obstacles and hindrances that have gotten in their way, you realize that they must not have a clear answer to what God would have them do. That person doesn't look at his daily work as God's task for him and feels no obligation to be obedient in his work. Every one of life's duties has a purpose. They are used to help you mature in your Christian life.

19

Is your life full of difficulties and temptations? Then be happy, for when the way is rough, your patience has a chance to grow.

JAMES 1:2-3

You need patience with yourself and with others, with those above you and below you, with those who love you, and with those who hate you; against sudden trouble; and under daily burdens. The weather may disappoint you; your body will get tired; your soul will need uplifting; you will fail in some of your daily work; and you will find that others will fail you. You have your definite wants, your times of sickness, your aches. Yes, you will experience disappointments, sorrow, injury, and delayed hope. Your troubles were small when you were a child, and in later years you may be called upon for greater sufferings. Patience comes through the grace of God, so you will be able to endure all things for the love of God. Commit *all* your ways unto God. He promises to direct your life.

20

I would have you learn this great fact: that a life of doing right is the wisest life there is. PROVERBS 4:11

No one has command over the circumstances which he may be called to bear. There are many powers beyond your reach—accident, death, good fortune, another's wrongdoing; these events may change in a moment. Do not look at these things as getting in your way. The Lord is stronger than all these things. Look at His Word, then the will of the Lord will be revealed.

21

In all you do, I want you to be free from worry.
I CORINTHIANS 7:32a

In this moment, cast all that concerns you onto God. Don't hold anything back. Lay yourself bare before God. Try to keep from being anxious about trivial things. If you commit these cares of today to Him, He will begin strengthening your faith for greater things. Give your complete self into God's hands; trust Him to take care of you. You are His child.

22

Why am I praying like this? Because I know you will answer me, O God! Yes, listen as I pray. PSALM 17:6

Whatever is bothering you today, tormenting your thoughts, tell God. Put the matter into His hands so you will be free from the things that give you great concern. He will take away your cares. You will become quiet and confident that you are depending on Him to help you in all ways. Put your cares and yourself, all your burdens, in the strong hands of God.

> Whate'er the care which breaks thy rest,
> Whate'er the wish that swells thy breast;
> Spread before God that wish, that care,
> And change anxiety to prayer.
>
> JANE CREWDSON

23

Lord, who shall abide in thy tabernacle? who shall dwell in thy holy hill? He that walketh uprightly, and worketh righteousness, and speaketh the truth in his heart. PSALM 15:1-2 KJV

Think of the things you are working toward. Do you have a reason to commit your life to these goals and work vigorously to attain them? There is a divine aspect to the work you are doing. When you do it with God in mind, you are presenting every act to God. If you do your work expecting nothing in return and are satisfied with your present work, you will be happy. There is no one who can prevent you from feeling you have done your best, and in doing so you have glorified God in your work.

24

I am the Almighty; obey me and live as you should.

GENESIS 17:1

Have you ever noticed that when you have made a sincere effort to faithfully follow the Lord, sooner or later several things inevitably follow? You experience the quietness of spirit in your daily life. You begin to accept the will of God as it comes each hour of the day. You become pliable in the hands of God in order that He can carry out the plan for your life's purpose; you are calm in the midst of rushing; your life experiences less worry or anxiety; you feel freedom from fear. These are all acts of grace from God, and they become the natural outward development of that unexplainable inward life which is hidden with Christ in God.

25

This is our God, in whom we trust.   ISAIAH 25:9a

Do not let your faults discourage you. Work at correcting them. Discouragement exhausts your body and causes you to commit more errors. Make it a practice to pray daily, whatever your work is. Then listen to the guidance of the Holy Spirit and do nothing but what He puts in your heart to do. You will become more relaxed; your words will be fewer but more effective; and in doing this, you will accomplish more good.

26

He will be gentle.   ISAIAH 42:2a

Every time you are called upon to suffer in this world, God is always there to help you endure all things. He shoulders your burdens and helps you accept them. If you will, in courage, completely submit yourself to God, no suffering is unbearable. Make up your mind that you will sustain a certain amount of pain and trouble as you walk through this life. It will help you.

27

Fear of man is a dangerous trap, but to trust in God means safety.   PROVERBS 29:25

God has brought you into "a time such as this." If you are not able to cope with the things He has prepared for you, you may find yourself unfit for any condition that might arise. Look at the things that give you trouble, and do not wish that this or that were not so. You may not be experiencing easy times. If not, perhaps you are being taught to stop depending on yourself. If believing does not come easy for you, you may have to concentrate harder and learn what belief is and in whom it is to be placed.

28

Being punished isn't enjoyable while it is happening—it hurts! But afterwards we can see the result, a quiet growth in grace and character.   HEBREWS 12:11

Were you annoyed with anything or anyone this morning? Did you hear words that upset your spirit? Did you feel any disappointments in any work you tried to perform today? Remember that from all of these will come the good pleasure of His goodness and afterwards, peaceable fruit. If you do not choke the deed or what may seem a frustrating experience, it shall blossom forth and ripen and make you a stronger person in this life. Walk the way of life that you know pleases God. Accept your state of being today.

29

No matter which way I turn I can't make myself do right. I want to but I can't. . . . When I try not to do wrong, I do it anyway.

ROMANS 7:18-19

As soon as you wake or as soon as you are dressed for the day, offer your entire self to God—your soul and body, your thoughts, your purposes and desires. Let these be what you feel would be His will for your life. Think for a moment of wrongs you may be tempted to commit through the day and go to your Father and tell Him:

Lord, I know you know that I am tempted in certain areas of my life, but I love you, and I want to stay completely away from the things you would disapprove of. I will earnestly try not to do an unkind act toward anyone, speak one idle word that could cause grief to anyone, give one envious look or dwell on one bad thought. If any of these temptations comes to me today, it is my desire to think, speak, and do only those things you want me to do. Lord, without you I am nothing, but with you I am everything. Amen.

30

God is love.   I JOHN 4:8b

Do you feel it is impossible, at times, to love a particular individual? It is easier to be polite or to show kindness toward those with whom you are seldom in

73

contact, or the one whose temper and prejudices don't rub against you, or whose interests do not conflict with yours than it is to keep up a steady self-sacrificing love toward those persons whose weaknesses and faults are always being forced upon you and are stirring up your own weaknesses and faults. Pray that in your weaknesses you may be strong and that God will help you love these who have, until now, only been irritations in your life. Commit even these to the Lord.

31

Yes, open wide the gates and let the King of Glory in.
PSALM 24:9

Your soul lies in the very kingdom of God. Since this is true, take thought and time to keep your life clean: "give your bodies to God." Try to live in peace: "he leads me beside the quiet streams." Keep your life clean from guilt: "he can be depended on to forgive us and to cleanse us from every wrong." By keeping your heart at peace, the temple of God can be pure. Keep your intentions right, then work, pray, and obey. Whatever God sends to you, be ready to accept it from Him.

32

She has done what she could.
MARK 14:8

Because you live in the presence of God, do at each moment what He assigns you to do. Do your tasks well and leave the rest without concern; it is not your business. Consider each duty as the work that God has given you to do and live in peace. Today, in this moment, try not to neglect anything He has given you to do.

33

The Lord is good. When trouble comes, he is the place to go! And he knows everyone who trusts in him!   NAHUM 1:7

There will always be outward circumstances coming your way in this world—good and bad. You will find the strength you need by trusting in your Father, and you will be satisfied with His will. Can anything really harm you? Can tribulation, distress, persecution, famine, nakedness, peril, or sword ever come between you and your Father's love? All the emotions you feel—love, peace, joy, all of these—will swallow up all bitterness and sorrow in your outward condition. He will give you the strength to do all things.

34

Many blessings are given to those who trust the Lord, and have no confidence in those who are proud, or who trust in idols.
          PSALM 40:4

Each morning try to organize your life for a calm day and remind yourself of this throughout your day. If something causes you to lose your composure, do not get upset or feel troubled, but gently go back to God and ask Him to give you a calmer attitude. Say, "I have made a wrong move; I'll be more careful now." Do this each time, and you will find yourself remaining calm even in upsetting situations. Remember these steps: do not become discouraged; be patient; wait and keep working to attain a calm and gentle spirit. This daily goal will make you a more effective person. Practice praising the Lord for all his goodness toward you.

VI

Service

Worship and serve him [God] with a clean heart and a willing mind, for the Lord sees every heart and understands and knows every thought. If you seek him, you will find him.   I CHRONICLES 28:9

1

I will bless the Lord who counsels me; he gives me wisdom in the night. He tells me what to do.   PSALM 16:7

Did you ever wonder whether God considered deeds or thoughts as great or small? Whatever He wills will be great to you, no matter if it seems small at the time. You do not have the right to measure the importance of *any* act. You may never know the joy you have missed by neglecting a responsibility that seemed so unimportant to you. If you will do your very best, one day at a time, you will never be left without sufficient help when large opportunities come your way. In this moment, tell God you want to give yourself to him, completely, then trust Him; continue to listen for his voice and go about your work, happy in the knowledge that God has enclosed your very life in His safe keeping.

2

The Lord God has given me his words of wisdom so that I may know what I should say to all these weary ones. Morning by morning he wakens me and opens my understanding to his will.

ISAIAH 50:4

Ask God to give you more sympathy toward others. At times you may have a desire to do something kind for someone else, but you never seem to get past that "good intention." There are numerous small acts that can be performed to bring some happiness into the whole day of someone who is ill. Put yourself in the place of one who is not able to get out of his house or even his bed, one who has fewer pleasures than you, and share a part of yourself with him. He may enjoy a new book, flowers, or a pleasant drive. Make it a practice of asking yourself, "What would I like for someone to do for me if I were sick or lonely?" Put that question into action; begin cultivating the habit of sympathy.

3

Anything is possible if you have faith.   MARK 9:23b

Impossible can never be in your vocabulary when truth, mercy, and the everlasting voice of nature are present in your life. When everyone else has said "impossible" and you feel all alone, then the possibility of any given situation has arrived. At that moment, do as you feel you should, whether it is in some form of action or is a decision; don't seek counsel from anyone else; let it be between you and God. You have great possibilities to the extent that you have the privilege of

78

seeking and knowing what it is God would have you do. Let no man keep you from your holy desire to please God and Him alone. With God all things are possible.

4

The important thing to remember is that our remaining time is very short, (and so are our opportunities for doing the Lord's work).   I CORINTHIANS 7:29a

Do you ever have the feeling for an urgency in living, that your life really is a "vapor"? Do not let misunderstandings continue in your life; do not let quarrels stay alive because you cannot find enough pride to be the first to say, "I'm sorry." Don't put off saying a word of appreciation or sympathy. Now is the time. There are some things that require your immediate attention because the time is now. Try, in this moment, to know and see and feel that your time is short, and it will keep you from neglecting things that must be done. Go immediately and do those things which you may never have another chance to do. "Whatever you do, do well" (Eccles. 9:10a).

5

Be kind to each other, tenderhearted, forgiving one another, just as God has forgiven you because you belong to Christ.   EPHESIANS 4:32

You have known people who seem to have a powerful way of living. You may have wondered what great acts that person has performed. Had he revealed his secret through his radiant smile and his good humor? Did he have a way of getting out of himself and learning to think of others? Maybe he knew how to bring quarreling people back together, visit the sick, and pray for others. He took time with little children; he helped his mate after an irritating day of work. He could see some good in each of his acts that only a loving heart could see. Anyone capable of great acts is the one who is always doing small ones.

6

Dear friends, let us practice loving each other, for love comes from God and those who are loving and kind show that they are the children of God, and that they are getting to know him better. I JOHN 4:7

If you choose, you can make the worst of one another. Everyone has his own weaknesses and faults. But you may also see the best in others. You may begin forgiving even as you would hope to be forgiven. You could put yourself in the place of others and ask yourself what you would want to be done to you if you were in their position. If you could only love what is lovable in people, then love will come back from them to you. Life would become pleasant instead of burdensome, and the earth would become more like heaven. You could become followers of His love.

7

That you will be filled with his mighty, glorious strength so that you can keep going no matter what happens—always full of the joy of the Lord. COLOSSIANS 1:11

It is not likely that you can always do great works, but you can always do something that is within your own daily responsibilities. You may be asked to be silent, to suffer, to pray when there is nothing left to do but pray. These are all acceptable to God. You may have disappointments, be contradicted in something you believe in very strongly, receive a harsh word unjustly, or be annoyed. A wrong received and endured as though you were in His presence is worth more than a long prayer. No precious time is lost if you bear up under all things in gentleness and patience, provided these things were not caused by your own faults.

8

For unless you are honest in small matters, you won't be in large ones. If you cheat even a little, you won't be honest with greater responsibilities. LUKE 16:10

Do you enjoy doing your own will? Do you want to do mighty things that would bring glory to your name? Do you thrive on recognition? Actually the greatest acts you can do are small things; so do them in the right spirit when God calls you to them: helping a lost child find his mother, doing an insignificant but thoughtful act for your family, writing a note to a special friend, inviting a lonely person into your home. God does not expect you to be faithful only on great occasions. Try to perceive how much your spiritual growth progresses through small obediences to Him.

9

This is our God, in whom we trust. ISAIAH 25:9a

Try not to be discouraged at your faults. Try to correct them. Put aside these strong feelings that exist in your mind. If you don't, you will find it literally exhausts your body and makes you commit more faults. Try to make prayer a matter of importance in all your daily work, whether it is in the home or in the business world. As you discipline yourself to God, say and do nothing unless the Holy Spirit puts it into your heart. If this can become a daily practice, you will become relaxed; you will speak fewer words and at the same time become a more effective person with seemingly less effort on your part.

10

For he satisfies the thirsty soul and fills the hungry soul with good.
PSALM 107:9

Every time you feel you are serving God in some way, you are enlarging your life to receive the capacity of love He has waiting for you at all times. Every time you pray you get rid of some of your unhealthy desires; you say a kind word to someone or perform an unselfish act, you patiently endure all things, you perform duties both great and small, you resist temptation—all because you pray. You are increasing the effectiveness of your life in order to more fully comprehend the endless capacity of God's love for you. Give Him each moment of your life (Eph. 3:19*b* KJV).

11

Be strong and steady, always abounding in the Lord's work, for you know that nothing you do for the Lord is ever wasted.
I CORINTHIANS 15:58

Have you ever felt that you have been faithfully striving for a goal and that you just cannot reach it? If you constantly aspire, don't you, in a sense, become elevated? If you will make the effort to keep your life right, God will give you the power to do more right. Give unselfishly and God will reward you with the spirit of giving more. Yours will be a fulfilled life, because the spirit of God's life is the sure blessing of giving. Love and God will give you the capacity to love more, for love is God's living within you.

12

What should we do to satisfy God?   JOHN 6:28

God's attribute of kindness is matchless. He puts every willing person in the place he would have him serve, and, in so doing, that one is truly about His father's business. He means that every chosen work for you should be delightful and satisfying. He gives you enough strength and enough sense for what he wants you to do. If you tire yourself or become frustrated, it is your own doing. Whatever you do, you cannot please God if you are not happy yourself.

13

I have spent my strength for them without response. Yet I leave it all with God for my reward.   ISAIAH 49:4b

> Because I spent the strength Thou gavest me
> In struggle which Thou never didst ordain,
> And have but dregs of life to offer Thee—
> O Lord, I do repent.
> **SARAH WILLIAMS**

If you feel that associates and friends around you are conducting their business and social life in such a way that you are caught up in a whirl which drains all your strength from you, resolve in this moment to live at a slower pace. Be called lazy, make less money, accomplish less work than they, and in every way be what *you* were meant to be. You have your own limits of ability. You are meant to do certain kinds of work. Be determined to keep your soul at peace. Work at it. Concentrate on it. Train yourself to do whatever you do calmly so you may always possess a peaceful heart. It is your best work that God wants, not the dregs of your exhaustion. He prefers your quality of work, not your quantity.

14

Continue to love each other with true brotherly love.

HEBREWS 13:1

Are you so full of cares today that you do not feel you have the strength to help another person? There is so much to be done. There are so many to be helped and comforted. These are the ones you must remain in contact with in your daily living. Try not to turn all your energy toward yourself, don't feel pressured by not enough time so that you will miss your turn for service and pass by that one to whom you might have been sent directly from God.

15

Do as you think best.

II SAMUEL 15:15*b*

If you are always ready to do what God appoints, all the trials and disappointments that come to you will never seem overwhelming because you realize they are His appointments. If He asks you to do a certain thing, hear and respond. If you have your schedule all planned for the day and He sends interruptions of phone calls and visitors so you can speak to them, offer encouragement or show some other kindness. Will you be aggravated because He has appointed you to bring glory to His name in this manner? If you have given yourself to Him today, why should you feel frustrated if His appointment for your day is to do some simple work with your hands or some errand that requires your time instead of seemingly more important work with your mind? Whatever He gives you, accept it graciously. It will help you have a better day.

16

May our Lord Jesus Christ himself and God our Father . . . comfort your hearts with all comfort, and help you in every good thing you say and do.   II THESSALONIANS 2:16-17

When you walk away from some work or some other person's need, saying you have too much concern of your own to be bothered, you may be severing the line on which a divine message is coming to you. You shut out the person, and you shut out the One who has sent that very person into your life at just the precise moment. There is always a plan working in your life. By keeping your heart quiet and your eyes open to needs, all works together. If you don't follow this thought, everything seems to fight together and goes on fighting until it finally gets right, somehow, somewhere. You are vital to the lives of those who stand in need and are virtually without hope. You are important to many people.

17

Oh, that we might know the Lord! Let us press on to know him, and he will respond to us as surely as the coming of dawn or the rain of early spring. HOSEA 6:3

And, as the path of duty is made plain,
May grace be given that I may walk therein,
Not like the hireling, for his selfish gain,
With backward glances and reluctant tread,
Making a merit of his coward dread,—
But, cheerful, in the light around me thrown,
Walking as one to pleasant service led;
Doing God's will as if it were my own,
Yet trusting not in mine, but in His strength alone!
JOHN GREENLEAF WHITTIER

By doing your daily work you learn to do it more effectively. Don't waste time arguing whether it is your responsibility or someone else's. Try to do what faces you, no matter how inadequate you may feel. You will begin to find strength to do things you felt you were not capable of doing. God will not ever ask the impossible of you. God accompanies each duty with the influence of His blessed spirit. Each performance will open your mind for larger intakes of His wonderful grace and will place your duty in total communion with Himself.

18

And you also are joined with him and with each other by the Spirit, and are part of this dwelling place of God. EPHESIANS 2:22

Throughout the world there is a temple being built by God. If you, a living soul, by free-willed obedience begin to catch the light of God's likeness, you become a living stone of that temple. When you are tempted, weary, and feel that life is drudgery, if you can realize the purpose of your being and give yourself to God, you give Him a chance to give himself to you. Your life automatically becomes a living stone for His temple. When your soul is being tried in any situation, realize that there God is shaping the pillars for His temple. If you could only have the vision of that temple of which you will always be a part, what patience you must have as you feel the blows of the hammer and know that a successful life comes about by letting yourself be made into whatever shape the master chooses.

19

And Enoch walked with God: and he was not; for God took him.   GENESIS 5:24 KJV

In these days is it possible to walk with God? Do you think you can walk with Him as you work, as you perform household chores, as you meet and talk with people? Can you walk with God when people annoy you or when you become weary from work or when the children are cross or when your plans for the day won't work out? Your religion may have a flaw in it if it begins to fail you in everyday trials and experiences. It must be a religion that is workable. It must be a religion that gives you strength in all things. If you will let God's divine love be conscious in your presence, there will always be an indwelling force with you that will lift you above *all* things.

20

You can keep going no matter what happens—always full of the joy of the Lord, and always thankful to the Father who has made us fit to share all the wonderful things that belong to those who live in the kingdom of light.   COLOSSIANS 1:11-12

It is not your problem to try to shape the total world's future; you are to shape faithfully a small portion of it. Each person is to try earnestly to find what his part is and then set out to accomplish just that. Do you have several duties to perform today? Keep these things uppermost in your mind and see that they get done. Maybe you won't get all of them completed. You might only finish one thing today, but you can be determined that you can and will do the others, too.

21

Grant strength to your servant.   PSALM 86:16

Practice letting God be the motive of your life, the measure of your being, the reason for your doing or not doing from morning until night. Then wherever you are, whether you are talking or being silent, if you are with others or alone, you are offering your life to the eternal Spirit that is in Him and from Him. Through the power and through prayer you will receive comfort, support, strength, and security. Let your main thoughts dwell on the fact that the only thoughts and cares you have are to be devoted to Him. Everywhere and in all things you will be his adoring, grateful servant.

22

So encourage each other to build each other up.

I THESSALONIANS 5:11

Who is your neighbor? Is it everyone with whom you have contact? First, your neighbor is literally the one who is next to you in your own home, your family. Then think of those who live in your neighborhood, on your street, in your town. With all of these, true charity begins. When you begin to genuinely love and show kindness to these, you have the beginnings of a true religion. Not only these, for the Lord teaches that your neighbor is also that one who crosses your path by changes and chances of life, that one whom only you can help, those whom no one else cares about. Pray for and see opportunities to help someone each day of your life.

23

Share each other's troubles and problems, and so obey our Lord's command.

GALATIANS 6:2

However troubled you may be about some question in your life, there is always this refuge for the moment. If you can't find the answer for yourself, you can at least do something for someone other than yourself. When you have a heavy burden, you might consider someone else who also has a burden and help him lighten it. When you think you cannot see God, you still have at your disposal the opportunity to show God to someone else. So remember this: there will be times when you cannot find help, but there is never a time when you cannot help someone else.

For the message to us from the beginning has been that we should love one another.   I JOHN 3:11

Have you ever wondered if, in your lifetime, you have ever accomplished anything really great? If so, remember, that in the hours of this day you can bring joy to someone. A kind word, sympathy, being considerate, being careful not to hurt a sensitive person, these acts cost so little, possibly your time, but they are priceless to the receivers. Hour by hour, moment by moment you can be a blessing to someone by performing an act of kindness. Kindness, practiced habitually, will give greater charm to your character than possessing a great talent or accomplishment.

25

Worship and serve him [God] with a clean heart and a willing mind, for the Lord sees every heart and understands and knows every thought. If you seek him, you will find him.

I CHRONICLES 28:9

> And if some things I do not ask,
>   In my cup of blessing be,
> I would have my spirit filled the more
>   With grateful love to Thee;
> And careful, than to serve Thee much,
>   To please Thee perfectly.

ANNA LAETITIA WARING

Small things come within your reach each day or hour. They are just as important to your spiritual growth as the greater occasions which occur. Faithfulness in small things—wanting to please God in great or small ways—becomes your real test of devotion and love. Aim always at one thing: to please God perfectly in small tasks, and attain a childlike simplicity and dependence. When you present your will before God, all hindrances will disappear; internal questionings will be dissolved, and once more you will be filled with a quiet peace and a sweet serenity.

26

All of us must quickly carry out the tasks assigned us by the one who sent me, for there is little time left before the night falls and all work comes to an end.   JOHN 9:4

Every time you put something off that needs to be done at a certain time, you feel burdened and begin to feel your duties are unpleasant obligations; you worry about it and lose your peace. Because of this you will find that you will not have time to do the work that needs to be done. This causes you to want to do it, simply to get it done rather than to do it well and enjoy it in the meantime.

27

Don't be afraid, for the Lord will go before you and will be with you; he will not fail nor forsake you.   DEUTERONOMY 31:8

In following this great promise, you can emancipate yourself from that anxiety that takes the joy out of living. It is a commitment that grants peace to you if you will accept it. It comes from the Supreme Being. Everything that is good has been implanted in your life by the Creator of men. It is a command in every moment and every condition of life that you are to do the duty that lies nearest you for that moment and that moment alone.

28

And he has put his own Holy Spirit into our hearts as a proof to us that we are living with him and he with us.   I JOHN   4:13

You will have sufficient strength for this day if you wait patiently, trust, depend, and seek God who promises abundant portions of His love, mercy, goodness, and majesty for your soul. Here is the secret of successful living. He will open all his eternal promises to you if you will, in turn, open your heart to His Word and His ever-satisfying spirit within you. Because of your natural, earthly spirit you may be tempted to become too eager and live at your own pace instead of staying with God's. Be patient, and wait for God in His own way and in His own time to do His work through you.

29

I am still not all I should be but I am bringing all my energies to bear on this one thing. Forgetting the past and looking forward to what lies ahead, I strain to reach the end of the race and receive the prize for which God is calling us up to heaven because of what Christ Jesus did for us.   PHILIPPIANS 3:13-14

Try making the best of what you are. Do not complain if you do not have the right tools for living, but use well the tools you have. What you are and wherever you find yourself is God's providential plan; it is God's doing. Take courage and live wisely by looking your disadvantages in the face to see what can be done with them. Your life can be compared with war: it is a series of mistakes. Neither the best Christian nor the best general can be judged by who makes the fewest mistakes. You become your best when you win victoriously by overcoming your mistakes. Forget all your mistakes and decide today to become victorious in spite of them.

30

Oh, that you would wonderfully bless me and help me in my work; please be with me in all that I do.   I CHRONICLES 4:10*a*

At the beginning of this day, offer to God all your desires of the day, the regrets of yesterday, and all those things that include home, friends, work. In this quiet time you will have pleasant memories, plans for your future, good intentions, work that has just begun. Think of the responsibilities you have for yourself and for others, and be ready to begin the work that is before you in this new day. The only way you can master the work that is yours is to offer it to God, and He will make all things right.

31

Yes, Father, for it pleased you to do it this way!

MATTHEW 11:26

Sometimes a person may indulge in an imaginary life: "Oh, if I only had more influence I could do great things"; "I could help more people if I had more money"; "I could be stronger if I didn't have so many temptations." Accept what God gives you. Begin counting all your assets. Concentrate on your limitations, and from these vast resources claim all that is good that you can use for His glory that will help you seek God's highest will for your life.

32

And so, dear brothers, I plead with you to give your bodies to God. Let them be a living sacrifice, holy—the kind he can accept. When you think of what he has done for you, is this too much to ask?   ROMANS 12:1

You may not feel that you have the mental or spiritual power that others have, but read the scripture verse again and notice that the living sacrifice is your *body*. This not only includes your mental powers, but it also includes offering a loving, sympathizing, encouraging word; running an errand for someone; working hard with your hands for someone else; taking opportunities as they come your way each moment of your days. You may not feel that your daily acts will ever receive worldwide acclaim, but always be willing to offer all that you have.